Why Are You Home, Dad?

Mary Harwell Sayler

Illustrated by John F. Ham

BROADMAN PRESS
Nashville, Tennessee

A Special Thanks

To my husband, Bob, and to my
parents, Horace and Mildred
Harwell, who were able to turn
their job crises into
new beginnings.

4242-76

ISBN: 0-8054-4276-6

Dewey Decimal Classification: CE
Library of Congress Catalog Card Number: 81-68925

Printed in the United States of America

A Word to Parents and Teachers

For most people, a job loss is a critical situation which affects the entire family unit. During the time of unemployment, the individuals may experience emotions which range from anger to guilt to despair. The unemployed persons may question their family's love and their own self-worth.

Children who are involved may feel afraid yet helpless to do anything about the problem. Because their viewpoint is limited, they may focus on events which seem unimportant to adults. However, children's needs and fears must be treated with respect.

Although all possibilities are not explored here, this book does provide an opportunity for children and adults to discuss their personal situation. The story is fictional, but it portrays some reactions and events which might occur during a job crisis.

Karen hopped off the yellow school bus. Behind her, Kirk jumped over the last two steps.

"Hey, Karen, Dad's car is here!" her younger brother shouted.

"He's home early," Karen said. She wondered why.

Inside the kitchen, Dad sat talking with Mother. From the looks on their faces, Karen could tell that something was wrong.

Kirk didn't seem to notice. He talked in a rush. "Hi, Dad. I'm glad you're home. It's warm out— want to play ball?"

Dad shook his head. "Not now, Kirk. Maybe later." The wrinkles in his forehead looked deeper than usual.

"Why are you home, Dad?" Karen wanted to know.

Dad sighed. "Something upsetting happened today. I need to talk about it with your mother first."

Karen knew that meant they wanted to talk alone. She did not like waiting, but this must be important.

"Come on, Kirk. Let's take an apple outside. When we're done, I'll play ball with you," Karen offered.

Outside, Karen munched her apple thoughtfully.

She wondered if she'd done anything to upset her parents.

Today her teacher, Mrs. Carson, had asked her not to talk out of turn in class. Karen didn't think Mrs. Carson was annoyed enough to call Dad at work. Still, she'd try to be quieter tomorrow.

"On no!" Karen thought. "Maybe the problem is Judy Henry. Maybe Judy complained about those dumb poster paints."

Karen was helping Judy with an autumn scene when she accidentally tipped over the orange paint. A big blob landed on Judy's *new* tennis shoes.

"Judy was so mad! Maybe she told her father," Karen thought. "And Mr. Henry is the manager in Dad's office!"

Now her younger brother called impatiently, "Come on, Karen. Let's play ball."

"I will in a minute," Karen answered.

"You said you'd play when you finished your apple," Kirk reminded her.

"Oh, all right." Karen agreed. She tossed the apple core into a clump of bushes for the birds. Soon they would welcome winter food.

During the next half hour, Karen and Kirk took turns batting the ball. Karen was ready to quit when Dad appeared on the porch. He looked serious. Karen's stomach fluttered as she hurried to the porch step where Dad was sitting.

"Can you tell us now, Dad? Why are you home?" Karen asked.

"There has been a cutback at work," Dad began. "I've lost my job."

"Oh, Dad, no!" Karen exploded. "That mean old Mr. Henry. It was only poster paint! Just wait until I see Judy. I'll . . ."

"Hold on, Honey. This has nothing to do with poster paints. Mr. Henry is sorry that I've lost my job," Dad said.

Karen protested. "But Mr. Henry is the manager. He hires people. He fires them too."

"Not this time, Karen. This is different," Dad said.

Kirk wiggled on the wooden porch seat. "I don't understand, Dad. Did you do something wrong?"

Dad smiled. "No, Son, I didn't do anything wrong. Business is not going well. My company does not have enough money to keep everyone who works there. If I stay on, I will not get paid."

"Will other people lose their jobs?" Karen wondered.

"I'm afraid so," Dad answered.

Kirk thought a moment. Then his face brightened. "Well, Dad, you can just find another job. Right?"

"Right," Dad said. But Karen thought he didn't sound too sure.

After that, Dad left the house every morning to talk with people who might hire him. But every afternoon when Karen and Kirk came in from school, Dad was already home.

At first Karen would ask, "Did you have any luck today?" But each time, Dad shook his head, "No." By the end of the week, Karen stopped asking.

Dad had insisted that Mr. Henry was sorry about the job loss. However, Judy Henry certainly wasn't. At school she seemed to enjoy pestering Karen. When other kids were around, Judy often asked, "Does your dad have a job yet?"

One day Judy said, "I've heard about those people on welfare. Are you living on welfare too?"

Karen felt like wringing Judy's neck! To make it worse, Karen didn't know the answer. She wasn't even sure what "welfare" meant. Somehow Judy made it sound terrible.

Since Karen couldn't ask her father, she asked

Mom, "Are we living on welfare?"

Mother looked surprised. "What made you ask that?"

Karen felt like crying. "It's that dumb Judy Henry. She is telling everybody at school that we're on welfare."

"Oh, Karen. I'm sorry," Mom said. She put her arms around Karen and gave her a squeeze. "I can't stop Judy from talking, Karen, but I can help you to understand. Would you like a snack while we talk?"

Karen wasn't hungry. Her chin quivered as she listened to what Mom had to say.

"Karen, your father is a hard worker. For many years, he had a good job. Some of the money he earned was spent. Some was used to pay taxes to our government. We also saved a little of the money," Mom explained.

"The money we have saved is not enough to pay for our home and food and clothes. We also need unemployment compensation," Mom said.

"Unemployment compensation?" Karen repeated. "What's that?"

"It is money that Dad receives because he is not employed. The money comes from the government.

It will help pay for the things we need."

Karen was beginning to see. "When Dad was working, some of his money went to the government. Now that he isn't working, he is getting some of the money back. Is that right?"

"Exactly! You have a quick mind, Karen. I knew you would understand," Mom said.

Mother's words made Karen feel better. She just wished that Judy Henry could understand, too.

During the next few weeks, Thanksgiving came and went. Instead of a huge turkey dinner, Karen's family had a small baked hen. Karen didn't mind too much. She was sure that everything would be back to normal soon. But the days dragged on and on.

Dad seldom went out of the house now. He never smiled or played games with Karen and Kirk like he used to do. Often he was grouchy.

One night at dinner, Kirk asked, "Can I have dessert?"

Kirk usually asked about dessert, but this time Dad was annoyed. "We don't have to have dessert every night!"

"I'm still hungry," Kirk insisted.

"Then have another helping of rice. It will be

thrown out if you don't eat it," Dad said.

"I don't want any more rice! I'm tired of rice!" Kirk said.

"Then you can go hungry!" Dad snapped. His face was getting red.

Karen wished her father would calm down. She wished that Kirk would be quiet. She didn't like the arguing.

But Kirk's voice rose. "If you had a job, I bet I could have dessert. And I bet I could have my allowance again and Christmas presents and . . . "

"Kirk! That's enough!" Dad commanded. "Go to your room."

Kirk pushed his chair back from the table so hard that it tipped over. "Dad, you're not even trying to find a job. You—you didn't even shave today!"

Kirk started to cry. He ran down the hall to his bedroom.

Karen sat very, very still. She felt sick. She couldn't believe that Kirk had actually talked that way to their dad.

"What's happening to everybody?" Karen wondered.

Dad sighed. "I feel like a *bum* when I'm not working! I guess I look like one, too."

Mother got up from the table and laid her arm

around Dad's shoulder. "Why don't you clean up while Karen and I do the dishes. When we're done, we can have a family talk."

Karen thought there had been too much talk for one day. She wanted to be alone. Instead, she stacked the plates and followed Mom into the kitchen.

Silently, Mom scraped the leftover food into the garbage disposal. Karen rinsed the knives and forks. She set them in the plastic basket in the dishwasher. She placed the glasses upside down on the top rack.

Mother broke the silence. "I was going to wash dishes by hand again. Then I learned that it's cheaper to run the dishwasher. I'm sure there are ways of cutting down on our expenses if we try."

Mother had never talked to Karen before about the cost of running a house. It made Karen feel more grown-up, but she felt scared too. She hadn't realized that the house cost money to run. What if they had to sell it? She didn't like the idea.

"Karen, would you finish the dishes?" Mother asked. "I'd like to check on Kirk."

Karen nodded. She knew what to do. When the dishes were loaded, she put powdered soap in the dispenser. Then she closed the door of the dishwasher. She turned the knob until she heard the water begin to flow.

Mother had not asked Karen to wipe off the kitchen counters, but she did. When she was done, she dried her hands and went into the living room.

Kirk sat close to Dad on the sofa. Kirk's eyes were puffy, but he had stopped crying. Karen was glad.

Dad spoke first. "Karen, your brother has apologized for his behavior. Now I want to apologize to all of you. I've been irritable lately."

"You have had a difficult adjustment to make," Mother said.

"That's true. But I am not the only one affected by my job loss. Kirk reminded me of that tonight. I guess I got angry because I do not want my family to have to give up anything—especially when Christmas is near."

Karen wanted to make Dad feel better. "It's OK, Dad. I have enough toys. And I don't mind giving up my allowance for a while. You will find a job soon." She hoped that saying those last words would make them true.

Dad said, "I'm afraid it's not going to be as soon as we expected. This close to Christmas people want to keep the jobs they have. I've been to every

company in town. There are not any jobs available right now."

"Will we have to move?" Karen asked.

"I hope not," Dad answered. Karen's heart sank. She wished he'd said no!

"I don't want to move!" Kirk protested. "Maybe I could find a job."

Dad smiled. "Thanks, Son, but you and Karen have your own work to do at school. There are other ways you both help."

"How?" Karen wanted to know.

"By having faith in me. By being patient. By doing without anything extra."

"What about shoes?" Kirk asked. "My tennis shoes are worn out."

Mother answered, "You will get shoes, Kirk, but they may not be your first choice. We will have to find the shoes that are the best buy."

"Will I get any Christmas presents?" Kirk asked.

"We will not have the same kind of Christmas, but your Mother and I will have a surprise. I think you will be pleased," Dad said.

Karen felt better after their family talk. But when she lay in bed that night, some bad feelings returned. She did not like the way everything was changing.

Karen was glad when Mother came in to kiss her good night. At least that hadn't changed.

"Karen, I know it is scary that Dad doesn't have a job. Yet it is exciting, too," Mother said.

"Exciting? How?" Karen asked.

"Because Dad may find another job he likes better. He and I pray about it often. We are sure that God has something special planned."

"Then why does Dad look sad?" Karen wondered.

Mother sighed. "Sometimes it is hard to wait."

The next few days went by quickly. Christmas was coming fast. Karen tried and tried to think of something to give Kirk and her parents. Without an allowance, she couldn't buy gifts. She could make something. But what? And what could she do for her teacher and her friends at school? Karen hoped that Mom would have an idea.

"I can't sew. I'm not good at crafts. I can't do anything!" Karen told her mother.

Mom gave her a hug. "You can do more than you realize. Your art work is nice. And you write lively poems."

Karen clapped her hands. "I know! I'll write poems and design a fancy card for each one. Then I'll give them to my teacher and friends."

"Good," Mom said.

"But I can't design a card as a gift for the class party. I don't know who will get my gift," Karen remembered. "The girls are supposed to wrap a gift for a girl, and the boys wrap one for a boy."

"Could you wrap something of your own?" Mother suggested.

Karen liked Mother's idea. In her bedroom she inspected her toys carefully. Most of them were worn or had missing pieces.

Mom appeared in the doorway. "Did you think of anything?"

"Not yet," Karen admitted. She held up one of her dolls. "She needs to go to the beauty parlor!"

"That's your favorite doll, isn't it?" Mom asked.

Karen nodded. "I wish she didn't look so sad. Her mouth is faded. Her hair is a mess. And her dress is stained."

Mother didn't say anything. She seemed to be thinking about something else.

"Karen, your books are in good shape. And a few of your records are not scratched. Will one of them do?"

Karen thought so. She looked through her shelves and took out the books and records which were in the best condition. Gradually she narrowed

down the selection to a funny record. Its bright cover looked brand-new.

At the school party, the record was a hit with the girl who received it. Karen's friends and teacher liked the cards she had made too. Mrs. Carson even read her poem aloud. Karen felt pleased.

Over by the punch bowl, Judy Henry stood alone, sipping her fruit juice. When Karen came for punch, Judy stopped her.

"I'll be getting a new Royal doll for Christmas," Judy said. "They're so expensive! Don't you hope you'll get one, too?"

Karen shrugged her shoulders. In past Christmases she might have wanted many things. This year, however, Karen had not even made out a list. A new doll did not seem important.

"I'm changing," Karen thought. Some changes seemed good.

Judy stuck her nose up in the air. "Oh, Karen! I guess you won't get anything for Christmas. Don't worry. I'll ask my parents to make a Christmas basket for your family. We always give a basket to the poor."

Karen's mouth dropped. She felt like smacking Judy's stuck-up nose.

"Judy, I've had enough of your big mouth! Just

wait and see how you like it when your father loses his job. And it probably won't be long," Karen shouted.

"You're just saying that to be mean," Judy shouted back.

"No, I'm not!"

"Yes, you are!"

Judy gave Karen a push. The cup of juice in her hand spilled onto Karen's blouse. Without thinking, Karen pushed Judy back. The remainder of the juice splashed all over Judy's clothes.

"Girls! Girls!" Mrs. Carson stepped between them. "You may not behave like this. Report to the office. Now!"

On the way to the principal's office, Karen kept her head down. Everybody was staring at her. She didn't want anyone to see her cry. She felt so ashamed. She'd never been sent to the office before, and now it was because of that Judy Henry!

"But Judy is right," Karen admitted to herself. "I did say those things about her dad's job to be mean."

Since school was almost over and Christmas holidays about to begin, the principal did not keep the girls long.

He spoke sternly. "I think it's appropriate for both

of you to miss the end of the party. While you gather your belongings, I will call your parents to come for you. Before you go, do you have anything to say?"

For once Judy was quiet. But Karen did not want to keep her bad feelings inside.

"I'm sorry I said what I did about your father's job, Judy. I don't think he'll lose it."

"Thank-you Karen," the principal said. Now his voice sounded kind. Judy didn't say a word.

Karen did not want to tell her father what had caused the quarrel between her and Judy. She hoped her mother would pick her up from school. But Mom didn't come. Dad did.

On the drive home, Dad asked Karen a few questions. Soon Karen told him the whole story. Dad listened carefully. He frowned when he heard about the problems that Karen was having with Judy.

"Honey, I'm proud of you," Dad said.

Karen was surprised. "But, Dad, it was awful!"

"I'm not happy about the fight you had with Judy, and I know you aren't either. But I am proud of you for admitting your part in it. I'm proud of you for telling me the truth."

Dad smiled at her. "Karen, I think our hard times

are helping you to grow inside. And do you know something else? I think this is going to be a great Christmas!"

The following week was a busy time at Karen's house. Dad often disappeared into the garage with orders for everyone to keep out. Mom acted mysterious, too.

At last Karen decided what she could give her family for Christmas. She rounded up colorful scraps of paper from her art box. Then she borrowed her mother's pinking shears. The shears made a pretty, scalloped edge around the paper.

When Karen had finished cutting out the paper, she wrote "COUPON" on the top of each piece. Then she listed jobs for which the coupons could be redeemed. Karen put "BONUS COUPON" on one piece for Kirk. Underneath she wrote, "This coupon entitles you to one cleaned bedroom." What a job that would be!

Karen slipped the coupons for Kirk into an envelope and wrote his name on the front. She did the same for Mom and for Dad. Then she placed the sealed envelopes on a low branch of the Christmas tree.

On Christmas Eve, Karen and Kirk helped Mother bake holiday treats. There was not enough money to buy the expensive ingredients for fruit cakes and date candy.

"Could we make sugar cookies, Mom? I like them best," Kirk said.

Mother agreed. "Karen, you may cut out the star shapes. Kirk, you may sprinkle on the sugar."

That night Karen's family went to a worship service at church. When they returned, they gathered around the tree in the living room. Kirk played "Silent Night" on his clarinet and only missed two notes. Karen lit candles on the holly wreath which she had helped Mother make. Dad read the story of Jesus' birth from the Bible.

Dad said, "Jesus was born in the place where animals stayed. I'm glad that we have a warm, pleasant house."

"I bet Jesus didn't have star-shaped cookies for his birthday," Kirk added.

"I like our tree. It's small, but it's the prettiest one we've ever had," Karen said.

Mother smiled. "We have much to be thankful for—especially each other."

On Christmas morning, Karen woke up early. She knew this Christmas would be different, but she felt happy. She wondered what surprise Mother and Dad had planned.

Karen didn't have to wonder long. Together she and Kirk hurried to the living room where their parents were waiting. Mom had turned on Christmas music. Dad had plugged in the tree lights.

There were only a few presents, but Karen didn't mind. Underneath the tree sat her favorite doll, looking beautiful and new.

Karen beamed. "Oh, Mom, thanks!"

The doll had a freshly painted smile and well-groomed hair. Her wardrobe was new, too—two dresses and a pantsuit. Karen recognized the materials which had been leftovers in Mother's sewing box.

"Did you see the surprise Dad made?" Mom asked.

Dad laughed. "It started out to be a jewelry box."

Now the smooth wooden case held scraps of familiar fabric, ribbons, and buttons. There were needles and thread and a pair of scissors, too.

"This afternoon we'll have our first sewing lesson," Mom promised.

"Oh, good!" Karen exclaimed.

She couldn't wait any longer to give her family the gifts she had made. She took the envelopes out of the tree branch where they were hidden.

"From me," Karen said.

Kirk was happy with the coupons. Mom and Dad were too.

"I can't think of a nicer present you could give us," Dad said. "This year for Christmas, you gave yourself."

Karen's eyes felt misty. Dad had been right. This Christmas was special in a way she'd never forget.

Before school started back again, Karen had learned how to make a simple doll's dress. Mother had also taught her how to sew a hem and repair a seam. Karen felt better about herself. She could do more than she had thought she could.

Karen wondered, however, if she could ever get along with Judy. She dreaded seeing her again. But the first day of school, Judy was waiting.

"Well, I hope you're satisfied," Judy began. "You really got me in trouble at home. My dad was so mad at me. . . . "

"I'm sorry you were in trouble," Karen cut in. "It won't happen again if you will leave me alone about my father's job."

Judy made a face. She didn't answer, but Karen hoped that she'd heard the last of Judy's remarks.

It was hard to tell if Karen's talk with Judy

helped or not because soon after that Karen's dad got a job.

"The work will not pay as much as I earned before," Dad told his family. "But the job is only temporary."

Karen frowned. "Does that mean this job will end soon?"

Dad's eyes twinkled. "Not exactly. You see, Karen, the job I was in before was no longer needed. So I decided to find out what work *is* needed in our town."

"We won't have to move?" Kirk interrupted.

"No, Son. Your Mom and I never wanted to move. But we were open to every possibility for work," Dad said.

"Oh, hurry and tell them!" Mom said. She sounded excited.

Dad was excited, too. "I really looked at the jobs in this town, and I discovered that more people are needed in computer work. I'm going back to school! I'm going to learn how to program computers. When I have learned, my job will change again. Then I will earn a better salary than I earned in my old job."

"That's great, Dad!" Kirk exclaimed.

"It certainly is. But remember—it will take a while for me to finish the computer classes. Can you wait for extras until then?"

"No allowances?" Kirk asked.

"A smaller one."

Kirk shook Dad's hand. "It's a deal!"

"What about your thoughts, Karen? You're being very quiet," Dad observed.

Karen cleared her throat. She tried to make her voice sound exactly like Dad's. "I'm not happy about the job you lost, and I know you're not either. But I'm proud of you for telling us the truth." Karen stopped and giggled. Then in her own voice she said, "Dad, I'm proud of *you*. But the next time you come home early, I hope it's to play ball with Kirk and me."

Dad gave her a big hug and said, "It's a deal!"